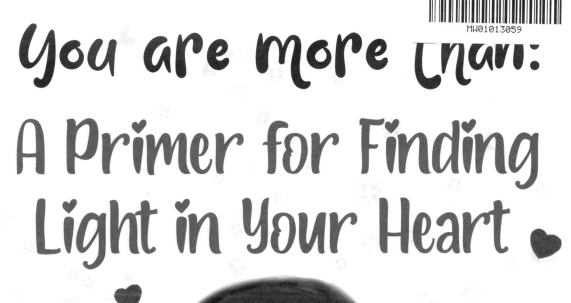

You are more than:
A Primer for Finding Light in Your Heart

Amy L.Stark,Ph.D.

Illustrated by Moran Reudor

You are more than:
A Primer for Finding Light in Your Heart

Amy L.Stark,Ph.D.

Illustrated by Moran Reudor

You are More Than:
A Primer for Finding Light in Your Heart

Copyright ©2022 by Amy L. Stark

ISBN: 9798838868121

This is a work of fiction. Names, characters, places and incidents either are the product of the author's imagination or are used fictitiously, and any resemblance to any actual persons, living or dead, events, or locales is entirely coincidental.

I wish to dedicate this book to Eileen Gaffen, my friend and publicist for over 40 years who always believed in me, to Jim and Linda for being in my prayer circle, and to the Masters for their education, love and guidance.

You are more than...
The things you have
The family you love
The sports you enJoy

You are more than...
The friends in your life
The place you live
The way you look

You are more than
your outer self.

You are more than
all of that.

You are...
The feelings of excitement
when you see a rainbow
A butterfly flitting by
The sound of the ocean

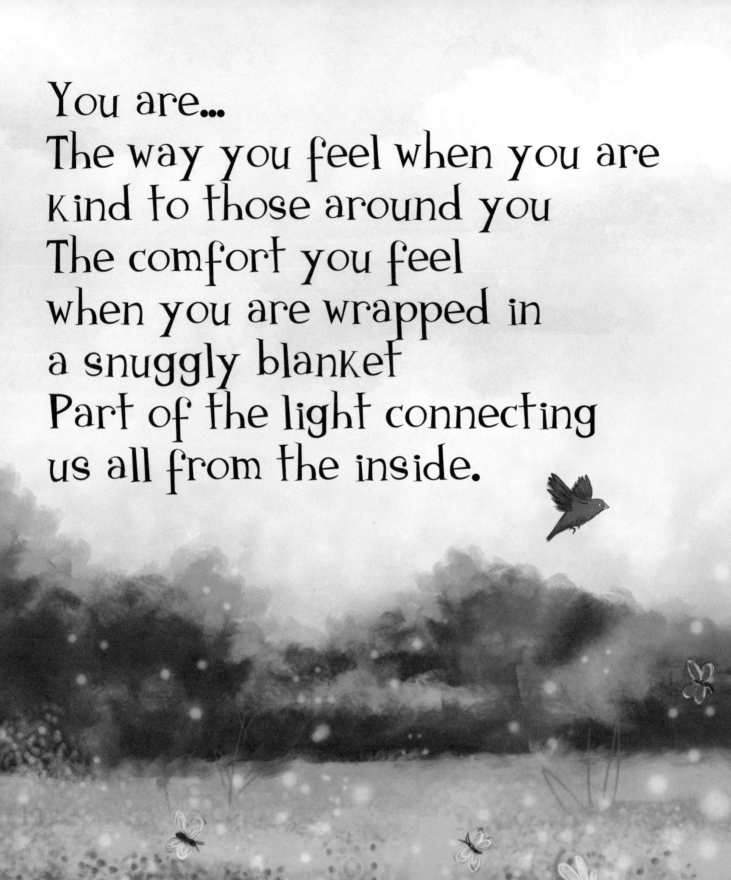

You are...
The way you feel when you are
kind to those around you
The comfort you feel
when you are wrapped in
a snuggly blanket
Part of the light connecting
us all from the inside.

Like holding hands in a big circle when you can feel your connection to everyone in it

It's the energy and
Joy you feel when you...
Help others and
are of service
Hug someone you love
Look at the beauty of
nature and see things
growing all around you

It`s the energy and Joy
you feel when you...
Notice the stars in the sky
and the moon at night
Feel the sun on your face
Breathe. You can connect
with the light inside.
Close your eyes.
You can see the light
in your heart

It's the energy and Joy
you feel when you...
Experience the positive
energy that comes when
you think of how
everything is connected.
Take a deep breath and
think of the blue sky and
the birds singing.
Feel the happiness
inside you.

It's the energy and Joy
you feel when you...
Feel connected
to the earth.
Reach up and connect to
the sky, the sun,
the moon and the stars.

Be the light
on the inside and the outside.
Find this energy when you
breathe and think about
the good things around you.

Be the light...
Love yourself Just
the way you are.
Love the light and
spirit energy that
is in everything and
connects all of us.

Be the light...
You are the light of love
everywhere you let it shine
When you feel the positive
energy inside you and
all around you,
you have found
something magical.
You are more than
what you have.
You are a part of
the magic and love we
can share on our planet.

Remember...

Breathe

Help others

Remember...
See the beauty of nature
Feel rooted to our planet
and embrace the stars

Remind yourself every day that
you are a part of the love on the planet.
Let your light shine everywhere you go.
Make a difference by knowing that when
you find your connection to everything,
you can find your purpose.
Because you are more than all that.
You are part of our connection to
the light and to each other.

Be the light.

Made in United States
Troutdale, OR
11/22/2023

14830289R00021